HEALTHY

AGING

Tips for a Vibrant and Active Life

Olivia E. Benson

CHAPTER 1

Understanding Healthy Aging

As we grow older, it is important to take care of our physical and mental health to ensure that we can maintain a vibrant and active life.

Aging is a natural process that we all experience, but there are steps we can take to ensure that we age in a healthy way. In this chapter, we will explore what healthy aging is, what factors contribute to it, and the benefits of aging well.

What is Healthy Aging?

Healthy aging refers to the process of aging in a way that maintains good physical, mental, and social well- being.

It involves making lifestyle choices that promote longevity, vitality, and quality of life. This can include activities such as exercise, healthy eating, socializing, and staying mentally stimulated.

Healthy aging is not just about living longer; it is also about living well. Aging well means that we can maintain our independence, remain active, and continue to pursue our passions and interests. It means staying physically and mentally healthy, and being able to enjoy life to the fullest.

Image by karlyukav on Freepik

Factors that Contribute to Healthy Aging

There are many factors that contribute to healthy aging, including genetics, lifestyle choices, and the environment. While we cannot control our genetics, there are many lifestyle choices we can make to promote healthy aging. sStaying physically active on a regular basis is crucial for promoting healthy aging.

- Exercise can help maintain muscle strength, improve balance and flexibility, and reduce the risk of chronic diseases such as diabetes, heart disease, and osteoporosis. For adults, the American Heart Association suggests engaging in moderate-intensity physical activity for a minimum of 150 minutes per week.

Image by rawpixel.com on Freepik

- Healthy Diet: Eating a healthy diet is another key factor in healthy aging. A balanced diet that includes plenty of fruits, vegetables, whole grains, lean proteins, and healthy fats can help maintain a healthy weight, reduce the risk of chronic diseases, and provide the necessary nutrients for optimal health.

Healthy Diet

- Mental Stimulation: Staying mentally stimulated is also important for healthy aging. Activities such as reading, playing games, and learning new skills can help keep the mind sharp and reduce the risk of cognitive decline.

- Social Connections: Maintaining social connections is crucial for healthy aging. Socializing with friends and family can help reduce stress, provide a sense of belonging, and promote mental well-being.

- Environmental Factors: Environmental factors such as pollution, exposure to toxins, and access to healthcare can also impact healthy aging. Living in a clean and safe environment, and having access to quality healthcare, can help promote healthy aging.

Benefits of Healthy Aging

There are many benefits to aging well, including:

- Improved Physical Health: Healthy aging can lead to better physical health, including improved mobility, cardiovascular health, and reduced risk of chronic illnesses such as diabetes, arthritis, and cancer.

- Enhanced Mental Well-being: Aging in a healthy way can improve mental well-being, including reducing the risk of depression, anxiety, and cognitive decline.

- Increased Independence: By maintaining good health and mobility, healthy aging can help maintain independence and reduce the need for assistance with daily activities.

- Stronger Immune System: Healthy aging can improve the immune system, reducing the risk of infections and illnesses.

- Better Sleep: Good health practices, such as regular exercise and a balanced diet, can lead to better sleep quality and duration, promoting overall health.

- Social Connections: Maintaining social connections and engagement in activities can lead to better mental and emotional health in aging individuals.

- Sense of Purpose: Healthy aging can promote a sense of purpose and fulfillment, as individuals continue to pursue personal goals and interests.

- Financial Stability: With healthy aging, individuals can maintain financial stability and security, reducing stress and promoting overall well-being.

- Improved Quality of Life: Healthy aging can lead to an improved overall quality of life, with greater enjoyment of daily activities and reduced physical and mental limitations.

- Role Model for Future Generations: By aging in a healthy and active way, individuals can serve as role models for future generations, promoting healthy aging practices and encouraging others to maintain good health practices throughout their lives.

Healthy aging is an important goal for everyone, regardless of age. By making healthy lifestyle choices, we can promote longevity, vitality, and quality of life.

CHAPTER 2

The Aging Process

All living organisms experience the natural process of aging. The aging process in humans involves physiological, cellular, and molecular changes that occur over time.

While the aging process is inevitable, the rate at which it occurs can vary depending on various factors such as genetics, lifestyle, and environmental factors.

In this chapter, we will explore the aging process, the changes that occur in the body with age, and the factors that affect aging.

How the Body Changes with Age

As we age, our bodies undergo various changes that affect our overall health and wellbeing. Some of the changes that occur with age include:

- **Decline in Physical Function:** Aging can lead to a decline in physical function, including muscle mass, strength, and flexibility. This decline can affect a person's ability to perform daily activities and lead to an increased risk of falls and fractures.

- **Changes in Cognitive Function:** Aging can also lead to changes in cognitive function, including memory, attention, and processing speed. These changes can affect a person's ability to learn and remember new information, solve problems, and make decisions.

- **Changes in Sensory Function:** Aging can affect a person's sensory function, including vision, hearing, taste, and smell. These changes can affect a person's ability to communicate, interact with others, and enjoy life.

- **Increased Risk of Chronic Diseases:** As we age, our risk of developing chronic diseases such as heart disease, diabetes, and cancer increases. These diseases can affect a person's quality of life and lead to disability and premature death.

Factors that Affect Aging

While aging is a natural process, various factors can affect the rate at which it occurs. Some of the factors that affect aging include:

1. **Genetics:** Genetics plays a significant role in the aging process. Some people may have genes that predispose them to age-related conditions, while others may have genes that protect them from these conditions.

2. **Lifestyle:** Lifestyle factors such as diet, exercise, and smoking can affect the aging process. A healthy lifestyle can help slow the aging process and reduce the risk of age-related conditions.

3. **Environmental Factors:** Exposure to environmental factors such as pollution, radiation, and toxins can affect the aging process. These factors can lead to cellular damage, inflammation, and chronic disease.

4. **Stress:** Chronic stress can affect the aging process by increasing inflammation and oxidative stress in the body. This can lead to cellular damage and an increased risk of chronic diseases.

5. **Sleep:** Sleep plays a crucial role in the aging process. Sleep deprivation can affect cognitive function, increase inflammation, and lead to an increased risk of chronic diseases.

6. **Social Factors:** Social factors such as loneliness and social isolation can affect the aging process by increasing stress and inflammation in the body. This can lead to an increased risk of chronic diseases and a decline in cognitive function.

7. **Medical Conditions:** Certain medical conditions such as obesity, high blood pressure, and diabetes can affect the aging process by increasing inflammation and oxidative stress in the body. These conditions can lead to cellular damage and an increased risk of chronic diseases.

Maintaining a Healthy Lifestyle to Slow the Aging Process

While aging is inevitable, adopting a healthy lifestyle can help slow the aging process and reduce the risk of age-related conditions.

Tips for sustaining a healthy lifestyle

1. **Eat a Healthy Diet:** Eating a well-balanced and nutrient-rich diet is essential for slowing the aging process. Give priority to the intake of an ample amount of fruits, vegetables, whole grains, lean proteins, and nutritious fats. Limit processed foods,

sugary drinks, and unhealthy fats to maintain optimal health.

2. **Stay Physically Active:** Regular physical activity is crucial for maintaining physical and mental health. Strive to engage in moderate-intensity physical activity for a minimum of 30 minutes per day, such as walking, jogging, or cycling.

3. **Manage Stress:** Chronic stress can have negative effects on overall health and accelerate the aging process. Develop healthy coping mechanisms, such as mindfulness meditation, deep breathing, or yoga to reduce stress and promote relaxation.

4. **Stay Hydrated:** Drinking enough water each day is essential for overall health and wellbeing. Aim for at least 8-10 cups of water per day to maintain optimal hydration levels.

5. **Get Enough Sleep:** Getting adequate sleep is critical for maintaining overall health and slowing the aging process. Aim for 7-9 hours of sleep each night and develop healthy sleep habits, such as avoiding electronic devices before bed and establishing a regular sleep schedule.

6. **Limit Alcohol and Caffeine:** While moderate consumption of alcohol and caffeine may have some health benefits, excessive consumption can be detrimental to overall health and accelerate the aging process. Limit consumption of alcohol and caffeine to maintain optimal health.

7. **Practice Good Hygiene:** Practicing good hygiene, such as washing your hands frequently and regularly brushing and flossing your teeth, can help prevent illness and promote overall health and wellbeing.

8. **Quit Smoking:** Smoking is a leading cause of premature aging and can have a significant impact

on overall health and wellbeing. Quitting smoking is one of the most effective ways to slow the aging process and improve overall health.

9. **Engage in Social Activities:** Maintaining social connections and engaging in social activities can have significant positive effects on overall health and wellbeing. Participate in social activities, such as volunteering, joining clubs, or attending social events, to maintain social connections and promote overall health.

10. **Maintain a Positive Attitude:** Maintaining a positive attitude can have significant positive effects on overall health and wellbeing. Develop a positive outlook on life and focus on the positive aspects of each day to promote overall health and happiness.

In essence adopting healthy lifestyle habits is essential for slowing the aging process and promoting overall health and wellbeing.

By following these ten tips, you can maintain a healthy and vibrant lifestyle well into your golden years.

The Importance of Nutrition for Healthy Aging

Nutrition plays a crucial role in maintaining health and wellness, especially as we age.
Our nutritional needs evolve as our bodies undergo changes.

It's important to understand the essential nutrients and dietary guidelines for healthy aging to maintain a vibrant and active life.

Essential Nutrients for Healthy Aging

- **Protein**

As we age, our bodies tend to lose muscle mass and strength, which can lead to a decline in overall physical function. Muscle mass is built and maintained with the aid of an indispensable nutrient called protein.

According to the Academy of Nutrition and Dietetics, adults over the age of 50 need at least 1 gram of protein per kilogram of body weight per day to maintain muscle mass and prevent muscle loss. Some examples of protein-rich foods that are considered healthy include lean meats, poultry, fish, eggs, legumes, and nuts.

- **Calcium and Vitamin D**

Calcium and vitamin D are important for maintaining strong bones, which can become brittle and fragile as we age. The recommended daily intake of calcium for adults over the age of 50 is 1,200 milligrams per day, while the recommended daily intake of vitamin D is 600 to 800 international units per day. Foods rich in calcium include dairy items, green leafy vegetables, and fortified products like cereal and orange juice. One can get Vitamin D from exposure to sunlight, fortified foods, and taking supplements.

- **Fiber**

Fiber is an essential nutrient for maintaining digestive health, which can become more challenging as we age. According to the Academy of Nutrition and Dietetics, adults over the age of 50 need at least 25 grams of fiber per day for women and 38 grams per day for men. There are several foods that are rich in fiber, such as whole grains, fruits, vegetables, beans, and nuts.

- **Omega-3 Fatty Acids**

Omega-3 fatty acids are essential nutrients that help to protect the heart and brain, which can be vulnerable to age-related decline.

The recommended daily intake of omega-3 fatty acids is 1.1 to 1.6 grams per day for women and 1.6 to 2.2 grams per day for men. Some foods that are rich in omega-3 fatty acids are salmon, tuna, walnuts, flaxseed, and chia seeds.

Dietary Guidelines for Healthy Aging

In addition to essential nutrients, dietary guidelines are also important for maintaining health and wellness as we age. The following guidelines can help promote healthy aging:

- Eat a variety of nutrient-dense foods. Foods that are nutrient-dense contain a significant amount of essential nutrients while being relatively low in calories. Good examples include fruits, vegetables, whole grains, lean proteins, and low-fat dairy products.

- Limit empty calories. Empty calories are those that provide calories but few essential nutrients. Examples include sugary drinks, desserts, and processed snacks. Limiting these foods can help maintain a healthy weight and prevent chronic diseases.

- Choose healthy fats. Healthy fats, such as those found in olive oil, nuts, and fatty fish, can help protect the heart and brain. It is advisable to steer clear of trans fats that are commonly present in a variety of processed foods.

It is advisable to steer clear of trans fats that are commonly present in a variety of processed foods.

- Stay hydrated. Dehydration can be a common issue for older adults. Aim for at least 8 cups of water per day, and include hydrating foods such as fruits and vegetables.

- Practice moderation. While it's important to eat a healthy diet, it's also important to enjoy food in moderation. Avoid restrictive diets, as they can be difficult to sustain and may not provide all the essential nutrients needed for healthy aging.

Incorporating Healthy Eating Habits into Daily Life

Incorporating healthy eating habits into daily life can be challenging, especially when faced with busy schedules and conflicting priorities. However, there are ways to Plan ahead. Planning meals and snacks in advance can help ensure that nutrient-dense foods are readily available. One can save time during the week by preparing meals in advance or cooking in batches.

- Make healthy swaps. Simple swaps, such as choosing whole-grain bread instead of white bread or opting for baked or grilled foods instead of fried foods, can help increase nutrient intake and reduce empty calories.

- Be mindful while eating. Eating mindfully can help increase satisfaction and enjoyment of food while also reducing the likelihood of overeating. Make sure to enjoy the taste, smell, and texture of your food, and eliminate distractions like TV or electronic gadgets while eating.

- Stay social. Eating with friends or family can make mealtime more enjoyable and provide opportunities for social interaction, which is important for overall health and wellbeing.

- Seek guidance. Consulting a registered dietitian can provide personalized guidance and support for healthy eating habits. Moreover, they can assist in managing particular nutritional requirements or medical conditions.

By incorporating these strategies, healthy eating can become a sustainable and enjoyable part of daily life, promoting overall health and wellness for healthy aging.

CHAPTER 3

Exercise and Physical Activity for Healthy Aging

Exercise and physical activity play a vital role in healthy aging. Regular physical activity can help prevent chronic diseases, maintain physical function and mobility, and improve overall quality of life.

In this chapter, we will discuss the benefits of exercise and physical activity for healthy aging, as well as provide practical tips for incorporating physical activity into your daily life.

Advantages of engaging in exercise and physical activity to promote healthy aging.

- **Maintain Physical Function and Mobility**

  As we age, physical function and mobility can decline, making everyday tasks more challenging.

Regular physical activity can help maintain and improve physical function and mobility, allowing for greater independence and quality of life. This is especially important for older adults who may be at risk of falls and other injuries.

- **Prevent Chronic Diseases**

  Chronic diseases such as heart disease, diabetes, and arthritis are more common in older adults.

Regular physical activity can help prevent and manage these chronic diseases, reducing the risk of complications and improving overall health outcomes.

- **Improve Mental Health**

Physical activity has been shown to have a positive impact on mental health, reducing the risk of depression and anxiety, and improving cognitive function.

This is especially important for older adults who may be at increased risk of social isolation and loneliness.

- **Builds and maintains muscle mass**

  Exercise helps to build and maintain muscle mass, which is especially important as we age and muscle loss becomes more common.aw

- **Reduces risk of falls**

  Exercise can help improve balance, coordination, and flexibility, which can reduce the risk of falls and related injuries.

- **Improves bone density**

  Weight-bearing exercise, such as walking, running, and weight lifting, can help improve bone density and reduce the risk of osteoporosis.

- **Boosts cognitive function**

  Exercise has been shown to improve cognitive function and reduce the risk of cognitive decline and dementia.

- **Reduces stress and anxiety**

  Exercise can help reduce stress and anxiety, which can have a positive impact on mental health and overall wellbeing.

- **Improves sleep**

  Regular exercise has been shown to improve sleep quality and duration, which is important for maintaining physical and mental health.

- **Helps maintain a healthy weight**

  Exercise helps to burn calories and maintain a healthy weight, which can reduce the risk of chronic diseases such as type 2 diabetes and certain types of cancer.

- **Improves mood**

  Exercise has been shown to improve mood and reduce symptoms of depression, which can have a positive impact on mental health.

- **Increases longevity**

  Regular exercise has been associated with a longer lifespan and a reduced risk of premature death.

Types of Exercise and Physical Activity for Healthy Aging

1. Aerobic Exercise

Cardiovascular exercise, also referred to as aerobic exercise, encompasses any physical activity that elevates your heart and breathing rate. Examples of aerobic exercise include walking, running, swimming, cycling, and dancing.

According to the American Heart Association, adults should strive for a minimum of 150 minutes of moderate-intensity aerobic exercise or 75 minutes of vigorous-intensity aerobic exercise per week.

Image by svetlanasokolova on Freepik

2. Strength Training

Strength training, also known as resistance training, is any activity that uses weights, resistance bands, or body weight to build and maintain muscle strength.

Strength training can help prevent muscle loss, improve physical function, and reduce the risk of falls.

The Centers for Disease Control and Prevention recommends that adults aim for strength training exercises at least two days per week.

Image by prostooleh on Freepik

3. Balance and Flexibility Exercises

Balance and flexibility exercises can help improve physical function and reduce the risk of falling. Balance exercises comprise standing on one leg, walking heel-to-toe, and practicing tai chi, among others.

Examples of flexibility exercises include yoga and stretching.

Image by Freepik

Incorporating Physical Activity into Daily Life

Incorporating physical activity into daily life can be challenging, especially for older adults with busy schedules or limited mobility. However, there are many practical tips for making physical activity a regular part of your routine:

- **Start Small and Build Up**

If you're new to physical activity, start with small, manageable goals and gradually build up. For example, you might start by taking a 10-minute walk each day and gradually increase the duration and intensity of your walks.

- **Find an Activity You Enjoy**

Physical activity doesn't have to be a chore. Find an activity that you enjoy, whether it's walking, swimming, dancing, or gardening. This will help make physical activity a regular part of your routine.

- **Make it Social**

Physical activity can be more enjoyable when done with others. Consider joining a walking group, dance class, or sports team to make physical activity a social and enjoyable experience

- **Make it Safe**

It is always advisable to consult with your healthcare provider before commencing any new exercise program, particularly if you have any preexisting medical conditions

- **Stay active throughout the day**

  Look for opportunities to be active throughout the day, such as taking the stairs instead of the elevator or going for a walk during lunch breaks.

- **Stay consistent**

  Aim for at least 150 minutes of moderate-intensity exercise per week, and try to exercise on most days of the week.

Exercise and physical activity are crucial components of healthy aging. Regular exercise can help improve heart health, build and maintain muscle mass, reduce the risk of falls, improve bone density, boost cognitive function, reduce stress and anxiety, improve sleep, maintain a healthy weight, improve mood, and increase longevity.

Incorporating regular exercise into daily life can be challenging, but setting realistic goals, finding an enjoyable activity, making it social, staying active throughout the day, and staying consistent can help make exercise a regular part of a healthy lifestyle.

CHAPTER 4

Mental Health and Emotional Well-Being in Healthy Aging

As we age, it's important to not only focus on our physical health but also our mental health and emotional well-being.

Aging can bring about many changes and challenges that can impact our mental health, including retirement, loss of loved ones, and changes in physical health.

However, there are many strategies and resources available to help maintain good mental health and emotional well-being in healthy aging.

The Importance of Mental Health and Emotional Well-Being in Healthy Aging

Mental health and emotional well-being play a critical role in healthy aging.

Poor mental health can lead to a variety of negative outcomes, including depression, anxiety, social isolation, and cognitive decline. Emotional well-being, on the other hand, can lead to positive outcomes such as better relationships, increased happiness, and a greater sense of purpose.

As we age, it's common to experience a range of emotions, including joy, sadness, anger, and fear. It's important to acknowledge and express these emotions in a healthy way, rather than suppressing them. Additionally, maintaining social connections and a sense of purpose can help promote positive emotional well-being.

Factors that Impact Mental Health and Emotional Well-Being in Healthy Aging

There are many factors that can impact mental health and emotional well-being in healthy aging, including:

- **Social isolation and loneliness:** As we age, social networks can shrink, which can lead to social isolation and loneliness. These factors can increase the risk of depression and other mental health issues.

- **Chronic health conditions:** Chronic health conditions can impact mental health and emotional well-being, especially if they limit daily activities and social interactions.

- **Retirement:** Retirement can be a significant life change that impacts mental health and emotional well-being. It can lead to a loss of purpose and social connections, and can also impact financial stability.

- **Caregiving:** Caregiving for a loved one can be emotionally challenging and can impact mental health and emotional well-being.

- **Cognitive decline:** Cognitive decline can impact mental health and emotional well-being, as it can lead to a loss of independence and challenges in daily life.

Strategies for Maintaining Mental Health and Emotional Well-Being in Healthy Aging

There are many strategies that can help maintain good mental health and emotional well-being in healthy aging, including:

- **Maintaining social connections:** Maintaining social connections can help prevent social isolation and loneliness, and can promote positive emotional well-being. This can include volunteering, joining a club or group, or simply spending time with family and friends.

- **Practicing self-care:** Practicing self-care, such as getting enough sleep, eating a healthy diet, and engaging in physical activity, can help promote positive emotional well-being.

- **Seeking support:** Seeking support from a mental health professional or support group can be helpful in managing stress, depression, and other mental health issues.

- **Engaging in meaningful activities:** Engaging in meaningful activities, such as volunteering, can help promote a sense of purpose and positive emotional well-being.

- **Managing chronic health conditions:** Managing chronic health conditions, such as through medication, physical therapy, or lifestyle changes, can help improve mental health and emotional well-being.

- **Fostering creativity:** Fostering creativity, such as through art or music, can promote positive emotional well-being and help manage stress.

- **Practicing mindfulness:** Practicing mindfulness, such as through meditation or yoga, can help manage stress and promote positive emotional well-being.

- **Embracing technology:** Embracing technology, such as video chat or social media, can help maintain social connections and prevent social isolation.

- **Seeking purpose:** Seeking purpose, such as through volunteering or taking on a new hobby, can help promote positive emotional well-being and a sense of fulfillment

CHAPTER 5

Maintaining Brain Health

As we age, our cognitive abilities may decline, affecting our memory, decision-making, and overall brain function. However, there are ways to maintain and improve brain health, which can lead to a higher quality of life and increased independence as we age. We will discuss the importance of brain health, tips for keeping the brain sharp, and cognitive activities and brain exercises that can help maintain cognitive function.

Importance of Brain Health

Responsible for regulating all bodily functions and processes, the brain is the most intricate organ in the human body. As we age, the brain undergoes changes that can affect cognitive function, including a decline in the number of neurons, changes in the structure and function of brain cells, and decreased blood flow to the brain. These changes can lead to cognitive decline, including memory loss, decreased attention and concentration, and reduced decision-making abilities.

Maintaining brain health is important for overall health and well-being. A healthy brain can help prevent or delay the onset of cognitive decline and neurological diseases, such as Alzheimer's and Parkinson's disease. In addition, maintaining cognitive function can lead to increased independence and a higher quality of life in older adults.

Tips for Keeping the Brain Sharp

There are several lifestyle factors that can contribute to maintaining brain health and cognitive function:

- **Physical activity:** Regular exercise has been shown to improve brain function, including memory and attention. Exercise also helps increase blood flow to the brain, which can help maintain cognitive function.

- **Healthy diet:** Eating a healthy diet, including fruits, vegetables, whole grains, and lean proteins, can provide the essential nutrients and antioxidants needed to maintain brain health. Certain nutrients, such as omega-3 fatty acids, have been shown to improve brain function and reduce the risk of cognitive decline.

- **Social engagement:** Maintaining social connections and engaging in social activities can help maintain cognitive function and prevent social isolation, which has been linked to cognitive decline.

- **Mental stimulation:** Engaging in mentally stimulating activities, such as reading, puzzles, and learning new skills, can help maintain cognitive function and improve brain health.

- **Sleep:** Getting enough sleep is important for overall health and can help improve cognitive function. Sleep is necessary for the brain to process and consolidate information, and a lack of sleep can lead to cognitive impairment.

Cognitive Activities and Brain Exercises

In addition to lifestyle factors, engaging in cognitive activities and brain exercises can help maintain and improve cognitive function. The following are examples of cognitive activities and brain exercises that can help maintain brain health:

- Reading: Reading can help improve cognitive function by engaging the brain in visual and mental imagery, memory recall, and attention.

- Puzzles and games: Engaging in puzzles and games, such as crossword puzzles, Sudoku, and chess, can help improve memory, attention, and problem-solving skills.

- Learning a new skill: Learning a new skill, such as a language or a musical instrument, can help improve cognitive function by challenging the brain and promoting neural plasticity.

- Meditation: Meditation has been shown to improve cognitive function and reduce the risk of cognitive decline. Meditation can help reduce stress and anxiety, which can contribute to cognitive impairment.

- Brain training programs: Several brain training programs, such as Lumosity and BrainHQ, have been developed to improve cognitive function. These programs typically involve engaging in computer-based tasks that challenge memory, attention, and problem-solving skills.

It's important to note that while cognitive activities and brain exercises can help maintain and improve cognitive function, they should not be used as a substitute for a healthy lifestyle.

Engaging in physical activity, eating a healthy diet, maintaining social connections, regular exercise and getting enough sleep are all essential for maintaining brain health.

It's never too late to start prioritizing brain health, and small changes made today can have a big impact on cognitive function and overall quality of life in the future.

Managing Chronic Conditions

As we age, the risk of developing chronic conditions such as diabetes, heart disease, arthritis, and Alzheimer's disease increases. These conditions can greatly impact an individual's quality of life and ability to function independently.

However, with proper management and treatment, many chronic conditions can be controlled and their negative effects minimized.

Common Chronic Conditions in Older Adults

Diabetes

Diabetes is a medical condition characterized by the inability of the body to regulate blood sugar levels effectively. Type 2 diabetes, which is more common in older adults, is often associated with lifestyle factors such as obesity and physical inactivity. Diabetes can lead to a range of complications, including nerve damage, kidney damage, and cardiovascular disease.

Heart Disease

Heart disease is a broad term that includes a range of conditions affecting the heart and blood vessels. As we grow older, the likelihood of developing heart disease rises. Coronary artery disease, heart failure, and arrhythmias are prevalent heart diseases among older adults. Heart disease can lead to chest pain, shortness of breath, and fatigue, among other symptoms.

Arthritis

Arthritis is a condition that results in joint pain and inflammation. Osteoarthritis is prevalent in older adults and transpires when the safeguarding cartilage that cushions the bone ends deteriorates gradually with time. Rheumatoid arthritis, an autoimmune disorder, is less common but can also occur in older adults. Arthritis can make it difficult to perform everyday tasks and can lead to decreased mobility and quality of life.

Alzheimer's Disease

Alzheimer's disease is a degenerative brain condition that impacts memory, thinking, and behavior. It is the most frequent form of dementia that older adults encounter. Alzheimer's disease can lead to confusion, mood changes, and difficulty with daily activities such as dressing and bathing.

Strategies for Managing Chronic Conditions

- **Lifestyle Changes**

Many chronic conditions can be managed through lifestyle changes. For example, maintaining a healthy weight, eating a balanced diet, and engaging in regular physical activity can help manage diabetes and heart disease. Exercise can also help manage arthritis by improving joint flexibility and reducing pain.

- **Self-Management Programs**

Self-management programs can help individuals with chronic conditions learn how to manage their symptoms and improve their quality of life. These programs can include education on disease management, strategies for dealing with symptoms, and emotional support. Examples of self-management programs include the Chronic Disease Self-Management Program and the Arthritis Self-Management Program.

- **Medical Treatment**

Medication can also play a crucial role in managing chronic conditions. For example, individuals with diabetes may need to take medication to regulate their blood sugar levels. Individuals with heart disease may need to take medications to manage their blood pressure or cholesterol levels. Medications can also be used to manage arthritis symptoms and slow the progression of Alzheimer's disease.

The Role of Medication in Managing Chronic Conditions

While medications can be effective in managing chronic conditions, they also come with risks and side effects. It is important for individuals to work closely with their healthcare providers to find the right medication and dosage to manage their condition effectively while minimizing the risk of side effects.

It is also important for individuals to follow their medication regimen as prescribed and to communicate any concerns or side effects to their healthcare provider.

In addition to medication, there are other strategies that can be used to manage chronic conditions, including complementary and alternative therapies. Examples of complementary and alternative therapies include acupuncture, massage therapy, and herbal supplements. However, it is important for individuals to discuss these therapies with their healthcare provider before trying them, as some therapies may interact with medications or pose other risks.

Other strategies for managing chronic conditions include:

- **Exercise:** Regular physical activity can help improve symptoms and reduce the risk of complications for many chronic conditions. It can also improve overall health and well-being.

- **Stress reduction:** Chronic stress can worsen symptoms of many chronic conditions, so finding ways to manage stress is important. Some effective strategies include meditation, deep breathing exercises, and yoga.

- **Sleep:** Getting enough quality sleep is essential for managing chronic conditions. It can help reduce inflammation, improve immune function, and promote healing.

- **Healthy diet:** Eating a balanced and nutritious diet can help manage chronic conditions and improve overall health. A diet rich in fruits, vegetables, whole grains, lean protein, and healthy fats can help reduce inflammation, control blood sugar levels, and improve heart health.

- **Social support:** Chronic conditions can be isolating and overwhelming, so having a supportive network of family and friends can be helpful. Joining support groups or online communities can also provide a sense of connection and understanding.

- **Regular check-ups:** Regular check-ups with healthcare providers can help manage chronic conditions and catch any potential complications early. It's important to follow recommended screenings and appointments.

- **Alternative therapies:** Some people may find alternative therapies such as acupuncture, massage, or chiropractic care helpful for managing chronic conditions. Prior to attempting any alternative therapies, it is crucial to consult with a healthcare provider.

Overall, managing chronic conditions requires a multi-faceted approach that includes both medical treatment and lifestyle changes. By taking an active role in managing their health, older adults can improve their quality of life and slow the progression of chronic conditions.

CHAPTER 6
Maintaining Social Connections

As we age, it is important to recognize the role that social connections play in our overall health and well-being. Staying socially connected can have a significant impact on our physical and mental health, as well as our quality of life. In this chapter, we will explore the importance of social connections and provide tips for maintaining and strengthening these connections as we age.

The Importance of Social Connections

Research has consistently shown that social connections are important for our health and well-being.

In fact, social isolation and loneliness have been linked to a number of negative health outcomes, including an increased risk of depression, anxiety, and cognitive decline, as well as a higher risk of mortality. On the other hand, having strong social connections can lead to a number of positive health outcomes, including improved mood, better cognitive function, and a stronger immune system.

Social connections can take many forms, including relationships with family members, friends, neighbors, and coworkers. These connections provide us with emotional support, companionship, and a sense of belonging. They also give us opportunities for social interaction and engagement, which can help us stay active and involved in our communities.

Approaches to maintaining connections with friends and family.

Maintaining social connections with friends and family members is important for our mental health and well-being. Below are some suggestions to remain connected:

- **Schedule regular phone calls or video chats:** Make a point to talk to your loved ones on a regular basis, even if you can't see them in person. Schedule weekly phone calls or video chats to catch up and stay connected.

- **Send letters or cards:** In a world where most communication is digital, taking the time to send a handwritten letter or card can be a meaningful way to stay connected with loved ones.

- **Plan social outings:** Plan outings with friends and family members, such as a picnic in the park, a movie night, or a game night. These activities provide opportunities for social interaction and can be a lot of fun.

- **Volunteer together:** Volunteering together can be a great way to give back to your community while also spending time with loved ones. Explore volunteer opportunities that align with your interests and values.

- **Attend family events:** Make a point to attend family events, such as weddings, birthdays, and holiday gatherings. These events provide opportunities for social interaction and help to strengthen family bonds.

Joining Social Groups and Organizations

In addition to staying connected with friends and family, joining social groups and organizations can be a great way to meet new people and stay engaged in your community. Here are some ideas for social groups and organizations to consider:

- **Senior centers:** Many communities have senior centers that offer a variety of social activities and programs, such as exercise classes, game nights, and social outings.

- **Volunteer organizations:** Look for volunteer organizations that align with your interests and values. This can be a great way to meet new people while also giving back to your community.

- **Interest groups:** Consider joining an interest group, such as a book club, gardening club, or photography club. These groups provide opportunities to connect with others who share your interests.

- **Community organizations:** Consider joining community organizations, such as a local service club or chamber of commerce. These organizations provide opportunities to meet new people and get involved in your community.

- **Religious organizations:** If you are religious, consider joining a local church, synagogue, or mosque. These organizations provide opportunities for spiritual connection as well as social connection.

Maintaining social connections is an important part of healthy aging. Staying connected with friends and family members can provide emotional support, companionship, and a sense of belonging.

Joining social groups and organizations can be a great way to meet new people and stay engaged in your community.

CHAPTER 7

Preventing falls and Injuries

Falls and injuries can be serious and even life-threatening for older adults. They can lead to hospitalization, loss of independence, and even death.

However, many falls and injuries can be prevented with simple precautions and modifications. In this chapter, we will discuss the common causes of falls and injuries in older adults, tips for preventing them, and home safety modifications that can be made to reduce the risk of falls and injuries.

Common Causes of Falls and Injuries in Older Adults

Falls and injuries can occur for a variety of reasons, but some of the most common causes in older adults include:

- **Muscle Weakness:** As we age, we naturally lose muscle mass and strength, which can make it harder to maintain balance and stability.

- **Medications:** Some medications can cause dizziness, drowsiness, and other side effects that increase the risk of falls.

- **Vision Problems:** Visual impairments, such as cataracts or glaucoma, can make it harder to see obstacles and hazards, increasing the risk of falls.

- **Environmental Hazards:** Slippery floors, poor lighting, and clutter can create hazards that increase the risk of falls.

- **Chronic Conditions:** Certain chronic conditions, such as arthritis or Parkinson's disease, can affect balance and mobility, increasing the risk of falls.

Tips for Preventing Falls and Injuries

There are many things that older adults can do to reduce the risk of falls and injuries, including:

- **Exercise Regularly:** Regular exercise can help improve strength, balance, and coordination, reducing the risk of falls.

- **Review Medications:** Older adults should review their medications with their healthcare provider to make sure they are not taking any medications that could increase the risk of falls.

- **Get Regular Vision Exams:** Regular vision exams can help detect and treat visual impairments that could increase the risk of falls.

- **Wear Proper Footwear:** Shoes with good traction and support can help prevent slips and falls.

- **Remove Hazards:** Removing hazards such as clutter, loose rugs, and uneven surfaces can reduce the risk of falls.

- **Improve Lighting:** Good lighting can help older adults see hazards and obstacles more clearly, reducing the risk of falls.

- **Use Assistive Devices:** Using assistive devices such as canes, walkers, and handrails can help improve stability and balance, reducing the risk of falls.

Home Safety Modifications

In addition to the above tips, making modifications to the home can also reduce the risk of falls and injuries. Some alterations that can be implemented include:

- **Installing Grab Bars:** Grab bars can be installed in the bathroom, near the toilet, and in the shower to help older adults maintain their balance and prevent falls.

- **Removing Tripping Hazards:** Removing tripping hazards such as rugs or clutter can reduce the risk of falls.

- **Installing Handrails:** Handrails can be installed on stairs, both indoors and outdoors, to provide additional support and stability.

- **Installing Proper Lighting:** Proper lighting can be installed throughout the home to improve visibility and reduce the risk of falls.

- **Installing Non-Slip Mats:** Non-slip mats can be installed in the bathroom and kitchen to prevent slips and fall.

Falls and injuries are a common concern for older adults, but many of them can be prevented. Simple precautions and modifications to the home can significantly reduce the risk of falls and injuries.

By following the tips discussed in this chapter, older adults can stay safe, independent, and active for years to come.

CHAPTER 8

Sleep and Aging

Sleep is an essential component of a healthy lifestyle, and it becomes even more crucial as we age. Unfortunately, sleep patterns and habits can change as we get older, and it can be challenging for some older adults to get a good night's sleep.

We will explore the importance of sleep for older adults, common sleep problems, and strategies for improving sleep.

Importance of Sleep for Older Adults

Having enough sleep is essential to preserve excellent health and well-being. During sleep, the body repairs and restores itself, and the brain processes information and consolidates memories. Lack of sleep can lead to a range of problems, including mood disturbances, difficulty concentrating, and decreased immunity. As we age, the amount and quality of sleep we get can be affected by various factors, including changes in our circadian rhythms, medication use, and the presence of chronic conditions.

Research has shown that older adults who get sufficient sleep have better physical and cognitive health than those who don't. Adequate sleep is associated with a lower risk of chronic conditions such as diabetes, hypertension, and obesity. It also helps to improve memory, cognitive function, and mood.

Common Sleep Problems in Older Adults

Many older adults experience sleep problems, including difficulty falling asleep, staying asleep, or waking up too early. These sleep problems can be caused by various factors, including chronic pain, medication use, and medical conditions such as sleep apnea.

- **Insomnia** is one of the most prevalent sleep issues among older adults. Insomnia is defined as difficulty falling asleep, staying asleep, or waking up too early, and it can be caused by various factors such as anxiety, depression, or medication use. Insomnia can have a significant impact on an older adult's quality of life, leading to fatigue, decreased cognitive function, and mood disturbances.

- **Sleep apnea** is another common sleep disorder that affects many older adults. It is a condition in which a person stops breathing multiple times during sleep, leading to decreased oxygen levels in the body. Sleep apnea is often associated with loud snoring and can lead to daytime fatigue, mood disturbances, and an increased risk of accidents.

- **Restless Leg Syndrome (RLS):** RLS is a condition that causes an uncomfortable sensation in the legs, leading to an irresistible urge to move them. It can interfere with sleep and result in daytime fatigue.

- **PLMD (Periodic Limb Movement Disorder)** is a sleep disorder characterized by the involuntary jerking or twitching of a person's legs during sleep. This can disturb sleep and cause fatigue during the day.

- **Circadian Rhythm Disorders:** Circadian rhythm disorders are conditions in which a person's internal clock is disrupted, causing sleep disturbances. Examples include jet lag, shift work disorder, and delayed sleep-wake phase disorder.

- **Sleepwalking:** Sleepwalking is a condition in which a person walks or performs other activities while still asleep.

- **Nightmares:** Nightmares are vivid and disturbing dreams that can disrupt sleep and cause anxiety or fear.

- **REM Sleep Behavior Disorder (RBD):** RBD is a condition in which a person acts out their dreams during REM sleep. This can be dangerous and cause injuries to the person or their bed partner.

- **Bruxism:** Bruxism is a condition in which a person grinds or clenches their teeth during sleep. It can cause jaw pain, headaches, and dental problems.

- **Narcolepsy:** Narcolepsy is a chronic neurological disorder that causes excessive daytime sleepiness and sudden sleep attacks. It can also cause cataplexy, a condition in which a person loses muscle control during strong emotions.

Strategies for Improving Sleep

There are several strategies that older adults can use to improve their sleep patterns and habits. These include:

- **Maintaining a consistent sleep routine:** by sleeping and waking up at the same time every day can aid in regulating your body's circadian rhythm, thereby enhancing the quality of your sleep.

- **Create a relaxing bedtime routine:** Develop a calming routine before bedtime, such as taking a warm bath, reading a book, or listening to soothing music.

- **Make sure your sleep environment is comfortable:** Ensure that your bedroom is quiet, cool, and dark, and that your bed and pillows are comfortable.

- **Avoid caffeine and alcohol:** Caffeine and alcohol can disrupt your sleep, so avoid consuming these substances in the hours leading up to bedtime.

- **Limit daytime naps:** If you have trouble sleeping at night, try to limit daytime napping.

- **Exercise regularly:** Regular exercise can improve sleep quality, but avoid exercising too close to bedtime, as it can make it harder to fall asleep.

- **Manage stress:** Stress and anxiety can make it difficult to fall and stay asleep, so find ways to manage stress such as meditation, deep breathing exercises, or yoga.

- **Limit screen time before bed:** The blue light emitted by electronic devices can interfere with sleep, so try to avoid using electronic devices in the hours leading up to bedtime.

- **Avoid large meals and drinking too much fluid before bedtime:** Eating a large meal or drinking too much fluid before bedtime can cause discomfort and disrupt sleep.

- **Consider seeking professional help:** If you have tried these strategies and are still struggling with sleep, it may be worth speaking with a healthcare provider or sleep specialist to address any underlying issues.

Sleep is an essential component of a healthy lifestyle, and it becomes even more crucial as we age. Many older adults experience sleep problems, including difficulty falling asleep, staying asleep, or waking up too early.

Fortunately, there are several strategies that older adults can use to improve their sleep patterns and habits, including maintaining a regular sleep schedule, creating a comfortable sleep environment, exercising regularly, managing stress, and avoiding napping. If you are experiencing sleep problems, talk to your healthcare provider to identify any underlying medical conditions or medication side effects that may be contributing to your sleep difficulties.

Healthy Habits for Life

As we age, it becomes increasingly important to maintain healthy habits in order to live a happy and fulfilling life. The habits we form in our youth and middle age can have a profound impact on our health and wellbeing in our later years.

In this chapter, we'll explore some strategies for maintaining healthy habits as we age, and offer some tips for staying motivated and committed to living a healthy lifestyle.

Maintaining Healthy Habits

There are a number of healthy habits that are particularly important for older adults to maintain. These include eating a healthy diet, staying physically active, getting enough sleep, and managing stress.

- **Eating a Healthy Diet:** As we age, our bodies require fewer calories, but more nutrients. It's important to focus on nutrient-dense foods, such as fruits and vegetables, lean proteins, and whole grains. It is advisable to steer clear of processed foods as well as foods that contain high amounts of sugar and fat. Talk to your doctor or a registered dietitian for guidance on developing a healthy eating plan.

- **Staying Physically Active:** Regular physical activity can help maintain muscle mass, improve balance and flexibility, and reduce the risk of chronic diseases. Strive to engage in moderate-intensity physical activity for a minimum of 30 minutes on a daily basis, with activities such as walking, swimming, or yoga being suitable options.

- **Getting Enough Sleep:** Sleep is important for both physical and mental health. Older adults may have trouble falling asleep or staying asleep, but there are strategies that can help, such as establishing a regular bedtime routine, avoiding caffeine and alcohol before bed, and creating a comfortable sleep environment.

- **Stress Management:** The long-term presence of stress can adversely impact one's physical and mental well-being. Strategies for managing stress can include mindfulness meditation, deep breathing exercises, or engaging in activities that you find enjoyable and relaxing.

- **Hydration:** Drinking plenty of water throughout the day can help maintain good health, as it helps regulate body temperature, transport nutrients, and remove waste.

Image by Freepik

- **Sun protection:** Protecting the skin from harmful UV rays by wearing sunscreen and protective clothing can help prevent skin damage and reduce the risk of skin cancer.

- **Smoking cessation:** Quitting smoking can have significant health benefits, as smoking is a leading cause of many chronic diseases and can negatively impact overall health.

- **Regular health screenings:** Regular health screenings can help detect potential health issues early on, allowing for prompt treatment and better outcomes.

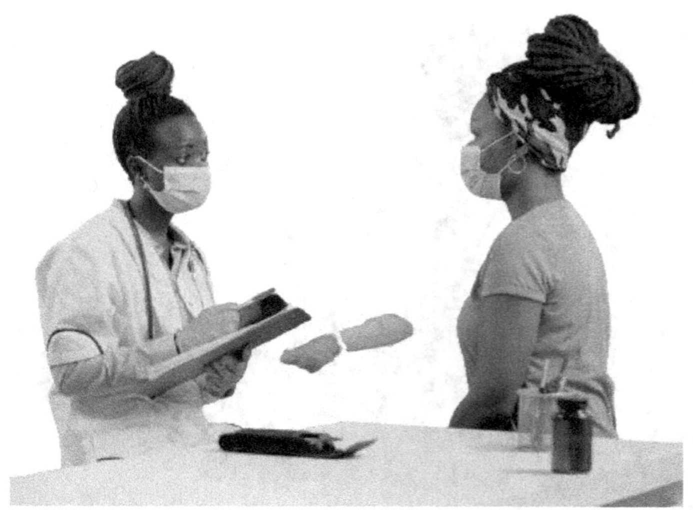

Image by DCStudio on Freepik

- **Social connections:** Maintaining social connections with friends and family can improve overall well-being and reduce the risk of depression and other mental health issues.

- **Self-care:** Taking time for self-care, such as engaging in hobbies, practicing self-compassion, and setting boundaries, can help maintain a healthy balance in life and reduce stress.

Self-care

Staying Motivated and Committed

Maintaining healthy habits can be challenging, but there are a number of strategies that can help you stay motivated and committed to living a healthy lifestyle.

- Set Realistic Goals: It's important to set realistic goals that are achievable, rather than trying to make drastic changes all at once. Commence with minor goals and progressively move towards bigger ones as time goes on.

- Find a Support System: Having a support system can be helpful in staying motivated and accountable. This can be a friend, family member, or a group of like-minded individuals.

- Monitoring Your Progress: Maintaining a record of your progress can aid in sustaining your motivation and visualizing the outcomes of your effort. This can be as simple as keeping a journal or using an app to track your exercise or food intake.

- Reward Yourself: Celebrate your successes along the way with small rewards, such as treating yourself to a movie or a new piece of clothing. This can assist in keeping you motivated and generating a positive feeling regarding the progress you have made.

- Be Kind to Yourself: It's important to be kind to yourself and avoid being too hard on yourself if you slip up or have a setback. Remember that setbacks are a normal part of the process and can be an opportunity to learn and grow.

Maintaining healthy habits is an important part of aging well. By eating a healthy diet, staying physically active, getting enough sleep, and managing stress, older adults can reduce their risk of chronic diseases and enjoy a better quality of life. Staying motivated and committed to healthy habits can be challenging, but with the right strategies and support system, it's possible to make healthy habits a lifelong part of your routine.

CONCLUSION

In conclusion, healthy aging is achievable by incorporating certain lifestyle habits into daily routines. These habits include staying physically active, eating a balanced and nutritious diet, staying socially connected, managing stress, and getting enough sleep. It's never too late to start making positive changes to your lifestyle that can help improve your overall health and well-being.

Regular physical activity, such as walking, swimming, or cycling, can help keep the body and mind healthy and reduce the risk of chronic diseases. Even a small amount of exercise each day can make a significant difference in one's physical health and mental well-being. It's also important to include strength and flexibility training to maintain muscle mass and joint flexibility.

Eating a balanced diet that includes a variety of fruits, vegetables, whole grains, and lean proteins can help support healthy aging. As we age, our bodies may require fewer calories, but it's important to make sure we are still getting all of the necessary nutrients our bodies need. Avoiding processed foods and excess sugar can also help improve overall health and prevent chronic diseases. Staying socially connected is also crucial for healthy aging.

This can include participating in community activities, joining a club or organization, or simply spending time with friends and family. Maintaining meaningful relationships can help reduce feelings of loneliness and isolation and improve overall mental health.

Managing stress is another important aspect of healthy aging. Stress can have a negative impact on physical and mental health, so finding ways to manage and reduce stress levels can be beneficial. This may involve activities such as meditation, deep breathing, or yoga. Lastly, getting enough sleep is essential for healthy aging.

Stick to a regular sleep schedule and create a relaxing bedtime routine to help promote better sleep quality. Avoiding caffeine and alcohol before bed, keeping the bedroom cool and dark, and limiting screen time before bed can also improve sleep quality.

Incorporating these habits into daily life can help improve overall health and well-being, regardless of age. It's never too late to start making positive changes to support healthy aging.

Even small changes can have a significant impact on overall health and well-being. In conclusion, healthy aging is not just about adding years to life, but it's also about adding life to years.

By staying active, eating well, staying socially connected, managing stress, and getting enough sleep, we can promote healthy aging and enjoy a vibrant and active life at any age. It's important to prioritize our health and well-being as we age to live life to the fullest.